GET ME OUT OF HERE!

GET ME OUT OF HERE!

EXIT STRATEGIES FOR ALL SOCIAL OCCASIONS

DAVID JACOBSON

D&C

David and Charles

A DAVID & CHARLES BOOK
Copyright © Elwin Street Limited 2006

David & Charles is an F+W Publications Inc. company
4700 East Galbraith Road
Cincinnati, OH 45236

First published in the UK in 2007

Conceived and produced by
Elwin Street Limited
144 Liverpool Road
London N1 1LA
www.elwinstreet.com

A catalogue record for this book is available from the British Library.

ISBN 13: 978-0-7153-2549-0 hardback
ISBN 10: 0-7153-2549-3 hardback

Printed in Singapore

Layout design by Roland Codd
Illustrations by David Eaton

Visit our website at www.davidandcharles.co.uk

David & Charles books are available from all good bookshops; alternatively you can contact
our Orderline on 0870 9908222 or write to us at FREEPOST EX2 110, D&C Direct,
Newton Abbot, TQ12 4ZZ (no stamp required UK only);
US customers call 800-289-0963 and Canadian customers call 800-840-5220.

Contents

PLAN A:

Avoidance is Better than Cure

The Art of Extrication or How to Say 'Gotta Go Now'

Introduction

THE GREAT MAGICIAN HARRY HOUDINI could escape from handcuffs and straitjackets, even while hanging upside down locked inside a tank of water. That's all quite nice, but the real question is – could he escape a blind date from hell? Or from a boring business meeting? Or from having to view someone's holiday pictures?

Indeed, could even the greatest all-time escape artist have gotten swiftly free from rude relatives coming to visit for an entire week? From dancing with egg-nog-emboldened Dave or Tina from Accounts at the office Christmas party? From the scene of an especially egregious one-night stand?

The reality is that awkward social situations can seem more difficult to get out of than a mere chain-wrapped trunk at the bottom of a lake. That's because our anxiety leaves us tongue-tied and unable to act. The first rule for getting out of any uncomfortable civil scenario is the same as for being bitten on the neck by a deadly cobra – don't panic!

Just kidding. Cobra neck bite? *Panic*. First rule of unpleasant circumstances? *Avoid them*. In these pages, you'll discover dozens of ways to dodge the venomous fangs of interpersonal obligation, from helping someone move to getting married. Some ploys are very situation-specific – the claim of a poorly fitting prosthetic leg makes an excellent excuse to avoid dancing, but a dodgy lip piercing that staples your mouth shut is more appropriate to begging off public speaking.

There are, however, some Universal Get-Outs. These specially marked passages include broadly useful and perennially popular ruses, such as 'The Hospital Visit to an Elderly Relative Excuse', 'An Attack of Food Poisoning' and 'Sudden Temporary Onset of Blindness'.

And, though rarely employed, there's always The Nuclear Excuse. This entails actually stating in brisk and succinct fashion why you really couldn't stand to babysit someone's creepy kids or attend another one of their grim get-togethers. Once you've dropped one of these pre-rehearsed devastating truth bombs, you'll want to exit the scene promptly!

So start with Plan A – the best excuses for getting you out of life's sticky spots. But if you fail to make timely evasive manoeuvres and you're already stuck, then it's time for Plan B – the very best escape routes: from creating a mobile phone scavenger hunt, to leaving a lousy party (especially your own), to getting out of your share of the housework by invoking faux feng shui. (Sure, some escape suggestions may seem a bit extreme; but would you rather give feedback on your neighbour's 700-page memoir of a life in the fastener industry?)

It's all here. So be sure to take this book with you to parties, work, dates or prison – any state of affairs you might want to get out of. This volume is the ultimate social insurance policy, the last word in life's loopholes and the one thing you can't afford to avoid.

PLAN A:
Avoidance is Better than Cure

Avoidance is Better than Cure

It's always best to skip awkward situations in the first place – whether it's entering an airport metal detector with multiple below-the-neck body piercings or dating someone who calls themselves 'an avid amateur chiropodist'.

Notice how simple preparation – checking your intimate metal jewellery in with your luggage and checking under 'C' in the dictionary respectively – could have helped you avoid stripping for strangers or a wretched rendezvous with a foot freak.

This section puts multiple options for opting out at your fingertips – from dodging dull dinner parties, through declining a drunken dork's dance request, to deflecting awkward appeals for advice. But the most important thing to remember is that, having selected your excuse, you need to truly commit to it.

Whether it's talking as if your jaw is wired shut to pass on a dinner invitation, pulling off a painfully expressive fake limp to sidestep the dance floor or quoting a few lines by German poet Rainer Maria Rilke ('Have patience with everything unresolved . . .') as a faux-wise forcefield against dispensing actual advice, you're the one who has to sell it. Remember, you can't spell 'avoidance' without 'avid' or 'diva' – or, indeed, 'canoe', but never mind that last bit.

Some readers may not feel completely comfortable making excuses, whether it's claiming past psychological trauma to evade your company's off-site team-building retreat or faking imminent childbirth to fend off prison time for speeding in a residential area. Perhaps, like many people who don't work in politics or advertising, you have a little voice deep down inside that insists: 'Purposely misleading other people is wrong!'

Would that little voice of yours actually prefer spending the weekend huddling for warmth with co-workers amid a winter camping 'limits-transcending exercise'? Or would it rather await bail in a tiny stinking cell with a crudely tattooed bunk-mate named 'Bone-crusher'? And really, if it's so righteous, what's the voice doing hiding 'deep down inside' anyway?

Yes, avoidance is always better – and now there's no excuse for not having an excuse.

⚡ Small Talk on Public Transport

You're trapped on a bus, train or plane next to some unbelievably dull person who is inviting you to join them in their shop talk, description of physical ailments and complaints *du jour* about the world, from pet political theories to incessant chatter about their work as a tinned goods distributor or industrial catalogue photographer. Here's what to do when a mellow trip threatens to become a slow-drip torture session:

➤ Taking out a newspaper or a book only offers lily pads for the leapfrogging small-talker – 'Never cared for that paper . . .'/ *'Get Me Out Of Here* sounds anti-social . . .' Instead, the firm insertion of earphones (see Fig. 1) is the new default mode for: 'It's been great, but I'm going to start ignoring you now'.

Fig. 1

Fig. 2

➤ No audio headset? A mobile phone is your next best friend (see
Fig. 2). Pretend annoyance at the interruption of your new
friend's *fascinating* commentary by a silent vibrating 'ring'. Then
employ the following dialogue: 'No, I didn't see it . . . It's *how*
many pages?! . . . Oh for heaven's sake, you'd better read it to
me'. Roll your eyes and give an apologetic shrug to your
silenced seat-mate. You're now free to do whatever you'd like,
occasionally mumbling into your phone, 'No, read me *that*
too, the devil's in the fine print'.

➤ Up to 3 million people worldwide have narcolepsy, which can cause sufferers to suddenly drop off into dreamland for a few seconds or up to several minutes at a time.* After explaining the situation up front, nod off whenever your prattling neighbour says more than three consecutive sentences (see Fig. 3). Jolt awake, mutter apologies and ask them if they wouldn't mind repeating what they just said. Continue until they're exasperated into silence.

Fig. 3

* Depending on your religious beliefs, faking an ailment like this could ultimately send you to a place where you'll be seated with the small-talker for all eternity. But perhaps you can make a charitable donation down the road to smooth things over.

AVOIDING SMALL TALK:
THE OTHER NIGHTMARE VENUES

IN A LIFT

➤ If someone interrupts your daydreams, back them off with wearisome quasi-profundities: point out that even the contextualized experience of vertical transport renders no objectively valid meaning.

IN PUBLIC TOILETS

➤ If someone tries chatting from the sink or adjacent cubicle, take a note from your wallet, extend it under the partition and say: 'There's no toilet paper in here, do you have change for a tenner?' This should yield an appropriately horrified silence.

AT WORK

➤ While an actual piranha-filled moat may violate company policy, you can still set up obstacles to keep chatty colleagues away: old wobbly chairs stacked with documents or open-jawed ring-binders give them no place to sit. Like the boiling oil dumped on medieval invaders, perilously perched cups of hot coffee may also ward off work-mates. Finally, programme your mobile to speed dial your office landline, generating a call that you 'just have to get'.

Attending a Friend's Play

Your artsy friend is great – except for the artsy part: *Waiting for Godot* staged at freezing bus stops/a gallery full of huge white canvases with tiny stick figures titled *Untitled #417-433a*/café rants delivered squeaky-voiced from inhaled helium to protest modernity's 'castration of the spirit'. Here's how to artfully evade their next invitation:

- By coincidence, your own play, opening, dance or reading is at the same date and time. Call this 'synchronicity' – it sounds artier.

- As a wry commentary on the preponderance of the bourgeois and the philistine in contemporary society, you're avoiding all art galleries, dance and live performances in favour of snacking in an armchair and watching shopping channels. You're hoping to get a grant so you can relocate to a museum and display your nihilistic anti-aesthetic 24/7.

- Decline by haiku: 'I won't be at your show, because your "art" baffles and/leaves me queasy'. Perform a dance: helpless amid their kitschy crap (foetal position) you break free (fists in all directions) and lunge (lunge) to freedom (cartwheels)!

- You can't wait to attend their performance! And wouldn't it be cool if you repeated all their lines right after they said them, making a crazy echo effect in the back of the theatre?

Use a fail-safe medical excuse:

- a) You've got a repetitive stress injury of the wrists and must avoid bravura art that evokes your rapturous applause.

- b) You've got a slipped disc in your neck and must avoid powerful performances that make you recoil from their bitter truths.

UNIVERSAL GET-OUT #1:
THE HOSPITAL VISIT TO AN ELDERLY RELATIVE

- In the poker game of invites and turn-downs, no card trumps this one. Just say your favourite great-uncle has fallen ill. The beauty of this imaginary aged relative is that little detail is required ('Apparently it's his spleen this time . . .') and they can be used repeatedly.

Giving Feedback on Someone's Magnum Opus

They want to know your 'honest opinion', 'gut reaction' and 'who you envision in the role of the stuttering nymphomaniac'. Is their book a bestseller? Is their music ripe for radio? Should they send their screenplay to Spielberg? It's too late to feign adult-onset dyslexia or fake your own death (a reasonable, measured response) as they hand you their CDs or 700-page manuscript (*A Paper Clip for Helga: My Life in the Fastener Industry*). Your other options:

➤ You'll be asked 'What was your favourite part?' So read a random pair of pages, then, when pressed, exclaim: 'It's *all* so strong, but I do love the scene where [insert relevant scene]'.

Rather than actually reading their tedious tome or clichéd script, your job is to cobble together generally nice things to say:

➤ This is writing of the highest order – the pages are absolutely sequential!

➤ This is so rich, I'm sure it would reward repeated readings/listenings/viewings.

➤ You *love* this. But you both know what kind of commercial rubbish sells these days: nothing but sequels, one-offs and 'escape' books. Certainly, *you'd* buy *several* copies, but you're not sure Joe Public will be capable of fully engaging in such a brilliantly idiosyncratic vision.

These fingernails on the blackboard of feedback will have them making up excuses to take their book/CDs/screenplay back and get away from *you*:

➤ '. . . maybe if you just switched the genders/races/ages of every other character . . .'

➤ '. . . What if the narrator suddenly got laryngitis and several chapters were just like (. . . . .)?'

➤ '. . . I know it's your memoir, but what if the main character suddenly realizes he's a leprechaun?'

➤ '. . . I know it's a concept album, but what if all the songs were about cheese instead of fasteners?'

Family Gatherings

It's Christmas dinner, Sunday lunch or a full-blown reunion. Once again it's time to face your relatives: bitter Uncle Ralph with his nasty political views; the dim cousins who keep trying to fix you up, even though you're engaged; the sibling-in-law rivals insisting that your income's a pittance or that you've sold out. Here's how to notify your next of kin you're going AWOL:

➤ You can't come because you're helping those without wonderful families. You're working in a soup kitchen, answering a crisis hotline or visiting the housebound elderly. You not only get let off, you put Uncle Ralph in his place and one-up your rivals.

➤ You can't make it because your new memoir about your horrible family full of hateful uncles, dull cousins and insecure siblings-in-law is arriving in bookstores. You're tied up doing media interviews and talk shows. You'll send them all signed copies of *Family Reunions with Satan's Minions*.

➤ If excuses fail and you're trapped again, start drinking heavily. Then, call several friends from the bathroom. They can show up and, with apologies to your relatives, perform an 'intervention', confronting you about your 'problem'. Later, at the pub, it's a full night of drinks on you.

THE TARTAN SHEEP EXCUSE

Being the black sheep is no longer good enough to get you driven from the flock. You've borrowed money and failed to pay it back? They forgive you! You ran with the wrong crowd, cheated on your ex or joined a loony cult? They accept you! These days families force you to work harder at becoming *persona non grata*. So choose one from each column to generate the sort of multi-dimensional obnoxiousness that will get you dropped from your family's invite list:

Column A	Column B	Column C
Carpet-glue sniffing	Identity kleptomaniac (compulsive credit card thief)	Oil company executive
Bobble-head doll collecting	Anti-pyromaniac (compulsive fire extinguisher user)	Global arms merchant
Incontinent for kicks	Saucy graphomaniac (compulsive ketchup scribbler)	TV weatherperson
Musk cologne overdosing	Rhinotillexomaniac (compulsive nose-picker)	Amateur kerbside pedicurist
Secret-language muttering	Helio-nyctophobic (fearful of both light and darkness)	Excuse-book writer
Sudoku cheating		
Urban rat-trap bait-snacking		

Public Speaking

For many, the fear of public speaking (technical name: glosso-phobia) is a terrifying ordeal worse even than the fear of bald mothers-in-law who are also clowns (technical name: pelado-pentheracoulro-phobia). But there are plenty of rational reasons to dodge speech-making: the risk of a work presentation gone horribly awry, drawing a blank during a eulogy or blurting out something inappropriate while trying to ad lib a wedding toast. The right excuses, spoken privately, might avoid public shame:

➡ Thanks to camcorders and desktop editing software, the most speech-o-phobic can give their talk to a non-judgemental audience of none, then just hit play for the crowds. You can even dub over the part where you get the hiccups. Just make sure there's nothing private on that video disc.

➡ If brevity is the soul of wit, it's also the thing that can get you out of most public speaking. Just make quick work of handing off speaking duties. This may come as a complete surprise to the person you're suddenly introducing, but if they wind up hemming and hawing then they are the ones who screwed up, after your elegantly pithy introduction: 'Thanks for coming, now I'd like to introduce someone whose reputation speaks for itself, my personal hero in this industry . . . '

➦ It only takes pointing at your throat, then clutching it to express pain – which any chimp can do. You simply can't go on. Add cherry-flavoured lozenges to impart a scary redness to the back of your throat.

➦ You simply can't give the speech because the only way you can overcome your stage fright is to picture the entire audience naked. And once you do that you become visibly aroused – very visibly. So you have to think of something non-arousing and by then you've completely lost track of what you're trying to say.

THE 'HOW DOES THIS SOUND SO FAR?'
NON-EXCUSE EXCUSE

Approach whomever requested that you speak and ask to run a few lines of your talk by them:

- **Eulogy** '. . . and so they abruptly left the mother/father of their kids for the very person who'd wind up cheating on them *with their former spouse*! But really, those were the *good times* . . .'

- **Wedding Toast** 'Soon after they met, the bride and groom both confided in me that the other person seemed like "a very short-term thing", in fact, they represented a "romantic compromise" they'd only make if they had *no other options* . . .'

- **Retirement Dinner Speech** 'So he said, "We'll just lift figures from the inventory column each quarter and put them into booked sales, take our performance bonuses to the bank and by the time the big boys are any wiser, we'll be retired . . ." '

- **Conference Keynote Address** 'To those who call our industry dull, wasteful, sloppy, incestuous and corrupt to the core, I say you may indeed have a valid point . . .'

Becoming a Godparent

Two close friends have asked you to be godparent of their baby. This is no time to wax sentimental and buy a 'World's Best Godparent' mousemat. Accede to this and you're signing up for decades of birthday parties, graduation ceremonies and babysitting 'opportunities'. Act now!

➤ You're honoured, but wouldn't their much more successful friend be a better choice? Someday they could help the kid out with their important connections.

➤ You're deeply moved, but wouldn't it be better to bestow this honour on their ne'er-do-well friend in honour of him/her being six weeks/days/hours sober? Showing your faith in him/her could be just the thing to help them turn their life around.

➤ You can't be Godparent since you're a strict existential atheist; but you'd be glad to show up in the child's life, like the hand of fate in a random and indifferent universe, to either dispense sweets or rap their noggin with a mallet.

Meetings at Work

Most workplace meetings seem designed to waste your time, sap your spirit or tell you what you already know. Do your employer – and yourself – a favour by leaving them to the agenda-shuffling company dead wood. Here's how:

- You're sorry but you have to be across town for a big meeting – potential new client, very hush-hush, hopefully you'll have good news for everyone next week/month/year. Thanks to laptops, mobile phones and Blackberries you could just lay low in a café across town, but it's best to go home for a nap so as not to be spotted.

- Thanks to laptops, mobile phones and Blackberries you can fill a seat at a big staff meeting while still getting your day's work done – typing and talking into your hands-free set. You can always pretend that you're avidly taking notes on the proceedings (for example, Announcement of Bring Your Trained Bird of Prey To Work Day – what could possibly go wrong?) or be creating a play-by-play podcast of the meeting for those travelling or based in the company's new Mumbai, Dubai and Antarctica branch offices.

➤ You've briefed lower-cost employees in that new Mumbai branch office and arranged for *them* to hold the meeting instead (that is, discussing your job performance and raise). Given the time difference, they'll be done tomorrow morning. As soon as you get their lower-cost meeting's minutes via e-mail you'll forward them to all concerned.

Generate a hubbub that will let you slip out. Your possible suggestions include:

➤ **a)** Replace the sexual harassment policy with training in Aikijujutsu, a Japanese samurai martial art – that way inappropriate behaviour is dealt with forcefully and on the spot.

➤ **b)** Require the board to undergo drug testing before they approve top executives' pay.

➤ **c)** Build company morale by using competitors' products as speed bumps in the employee car park.

The most sublime of get-outs is the fake food poisoning excuse. After all, it's a sudden onset, swift recovery, could-happen-to-anybody-anytime-anywhere sort of thing. Whether warding off unwanted advances ('Before you try kissing me, there's something you should know . . .') or escaping the office holiday party ('Could've been salmonella in my eggnog . . .'), it's the ejector seat par excellence. No need for a back story, no one will seek details of your intestinal pseudo-suffering.

➤ So if you're trapped in a new logo brainstorm session, it's time to grab your belly with visible distress (see Fig. 1) and head for the door.

Fig. 1

➤ Either take your laptop to
an executive toilette or
enjoy a lazy afternoon in
the park (see Fig. 2).

Fig. 2

➤ Return later, stalwart and stoic: 'Feeling . . . better . . .
what did I miss?'

Living Together

You've already got a toothbrush and underwear at each other's places. And it does seem wasteful to pay two rents. Your squeeze thinks it's time for 'the next level of intimacy', but you thought that meant sharing a fondue fork. When you're not ready to merge addresses, try these excuses instead:

◆ You haven't dated through the ups and downs of an entire presidential/prime minister's term. They don't even know your secret nickname for your *second* smallest toe. (Note: This may be less effective if you are residents in an old people's home.)

◆ How will you keep the sexy spark alive when you're routinely prying each other's hair from drains and overhearing gargling – or worse? And that's not even mentioning the fatal discovery that your darling is a compulsive wee-hours consumer of dog biscuits.

◆ You consider your beloved a 'neat freak' because they always have to 'see what's underfoot', don't believe that a fork with old food hardened between the tines has 'evolved' into a spork, or that what's under your couch is 'a really cool dust bunny hutch'.

➤ You've overheard them talking in their sleep and it *sounds* like they want to repaint your entire place in their favourite team's loud colours and/or put up girly lace curtains and a floral stencil wall trim. With that threat hanging over you, you don't feel your relationship would survive moving in with one another.

➤ There isn't room for them to move in (or vice versa), as you maintain a complete archive of all of your school sports trophies, school quizzes, work memos, stuffed pets and other memorabilia that you just can't bring yourself to throw away. You've got to think about that big museum they'll build when you're a famous historical figure.

➤ If word of your shacking up got back to your very traditional maternal grandmother, she'd disown you. And you're sure she's got a tidy sum tucked away somewhere – surely your beloved wouldn't want you to miss out on your inheritance by moving in together now rather than in, say, five years time?

Dinner Party Invitations

Sure, dinner parties offer the appeal of a fabulous meal, fine wine and convivial friends. But you've learned whose invites to avoid – the meal will be an experimental disaster, the wine an expectorant cough syrup and the conversation inane. For those, we've cooked up your excuses:

- It's your new boyfriend/girlfriend/spouse/child. They're severely allergic to nuts, seeds, shellfish, wheat, dairy, soy, sweetcorn, marshmallows, yellow food dyes E105 and E107, and the vowels e, i and u in alphabet soup. Even if they abstained, if *you* ate some of those foods and then kissed them, they could still break out in a deadly rash.

- You'd love to come, especially now that you're in training as a competitive eater. Technically, a *gurgitator*. You've been stretching your stomach by guzzling jugs of water and holding your oesophagus open so you can stuff down meats or pies faster without gagging. Ask what lubricants – you mean *condiments* – they'll be serving!

- Last time you went to a dinner party, you came home and caught the babysitter on the couch in a flagrant embrace with their squeeze. You crept back out and waited, but you fell asleep and only woke at 2 AM. Then they demanded overtime. You got in an argument and now they won't sit for you anymore.

THE NUCLEAR EXCUSE

- Remember, delivering The Big N.O. is like tearing a plaster off a hairy body part: you've got to work fast. Practise blurting out the following in a single breath:

'I can't make it to your dinner party because the average life expectancy even in the most advanced nations is about 80 years, which breaks down to 700,800 hours, and I'll spend a third of that asleep (subtract 233,600); and 40 hours a week for 40 years at work (subtract 76,800); then there's commuting and being stuck in traffic jams (subtract 23,400); watching bad TV shows and re-runs I didn't like the first time (19,200); plus bathroom time, flossing, and volunteer work (17,841). That only leaves 329,959 hours of life to really enjoy – so you can see I don't have two or three of those to waste on tasteless cuisine, cheap zinfandel and a gathering of negative-IQ mouth breathers.'

Getting Up and Dancing

There are lots of times you'd enjoy dancing, for example while home alone, wearing headphones and in your underwear, but not now: the music's painfully uncool, there's no one else on the dance floor and/or the person approaching you has the frothing enthusiasm of a lunatic exhibitionist. Without being anti-social, here are your anti-dancing steps:

- You'd *love* to, but you're recovering from a badly sprained ankle or a rupture of the anterior cruciate knee ligament (practise saying *anterior cruciate* so it rolls off the tongue).

- Of course you like to dance, but you've just never been able to get the hang of the Argentine Tango/Macarena/Hokey Cokey.

- Sorry, but you *promised* (look around expectantly) you'd save the night's first dance for [name of your favorite Disney animation character plus a brand of beer]. Perhaps later . . .

- Your latest fake leg doesn't fit very well. Sometimes it slips clean off, causing you to fall and hit your head – again.

→ You'd love to dance, just not to this song. It was playing in the background when you lost your virginity, so it would feel too weird. (Bonus points if the song is *The Hokey Cokey*, *YMCA*, or *I'm Too Sexy*.)

→ You'd love to dance, just not to this song. (This works best if you haven't already used the above excuse, but may be a back up if the same person approaches you again.) It was playing in the background when your best childhood friend was killed in a tragic [choose only one] clay pigeon shooting/body-piercing/mechanical bull-riding accident. 'I'd feel like I was dancing on his/her grave.'

Even the most attractive people are less approachable when they are dripping with perspiration . . .

Fig. 1

→ Before going out, pursue a vigorous aerobic workout (see Fig. 1). Try 20 brisk minutes on an exercise bicycle or visit a sauna fully clothed.

◆ This should leave you too slimy and reeking for even the person most desperately seeking a dance partner (see Fig. 2).

Fig. 2

◆ Normally, you'd love to but you're getting over an inner ear infection that causes nauseating vertigo and a tendency to fall over and hit your head – again.

◆ You've been told such vigorous motions could dislodge the blood clot in your leg, sending it to a lung. For best delivery, start to rise, muttering, 'Oh, to hell with doctors.' Then slump back, grasping your side: 'Probably . . . just . . . a stitch!'

♀ EXCUSES FOR HER

➤ Confide in a teeth-gritted whisper: 'I'd love to, but I have the worst PMT/pre-PMT/post-pre-PMT.'

➤ You're waiting for a faster- or slower-paced number. Always insist the rhythm is not quite right for you to take to the floor. You can always add: 'more syncopated' or 'more samba-esque' to further muddy the waters.

➤ Offer to go for a walk instead. Guys are suckers for this and really, you only have to walk him as far as the nearest bar or beer fridge. At least you won't have to dance with that loser.

♂ EXCUSES FOR HIM

➤ Confide your lack of underwear (it's a long story), so you'd run a high risk of injury.

➤ You've already had a few too many, and you're afraid that if you move too much, the room may start to spin and then who knows what will come up.

➤ The vigorous motion may cause your recent hernia incision to reopen.

Giving Advice

Your friend, neighbour and/or ex-cellmate wants to know if they should: a) quit their unfulfilling job; b) leave their not-so-great lover or c) sell their lame stocks to buy that alluring flat. You could tell them what they want to hear, but then you'll feel responsible if it all goes hideously wrong. Here's how to avoid giving advice:

➤ You're just too close to them to see the situation objectively. Add that you support them 100 per cent in whatever they ultimately decide to do!

➤ Should they dump their stock portfolio to buy an unseen pasture on the remote Mongolian outback that should appreciate as the world's appetite for yak milk grows? Pretend to think about it, arching one brow and tapping your fingertips together, then ask intensely: 'What do *you* think you should do?' Repeat until they're sick of talking about it.

➤ They say: 'But didn't you *also* quit your steady job selling fancy dress shoes and leave your longtime love for a prison escapee you'd only met on the internet?' You say: 'No, my situation was very different, I sold *casual* dress shoes.'

▶ Learn to say, as if it is just occurring to you, the lines of the
German poet Rainer Maria Rilke: 'Have patience with everything
unresolved in your heart and try to love the questions
themselves as if they were locked rooms or books written in a
very foreign language. Don't search for the answers, which
could not be given to you now, because you would not be able
to live them. And the point is, to live everything. Live the
questions now. Perhaps then, someday far in the future, you will
gradually, without even noticing it, live your way into the
answer.' Then add: 'Look at the time, my favorite reality TV
show is on!'

Just get it over with by repeating uselessly generic one-liners:

▶ 'Whatever you do, follow your heart.' Freely add, 'or
your pancreas'.

▶ 'You'll always regret the things you *don't* do.' If asked for
clarification, add 'plus about 57 per cent of the things
that you do'.

▶ 'Whatever you ultimately decide, don't second-guess yourself.'
If asked for clarification, add 'unless it's a total disaster'.

Helping Someone Move

It sounds mean-spirited, but this is a classic case of no good deed going unpunished. You'll be the only one to show up, then suffer through endless hours of disorganized schlepping. After spending your entire day off helping out, you'll be muscle-sore, dirty and depressed. Just don't do it:

➤ Fake an injury that prevents lifting. It can be a slipped spinal disc, a healing hernia or even a repetitive stress injury (damn these computer keyboards!) A 'pulled muscle' makes an obvious yet irrefutable last-minute excuse.

➤ You don't feel right taking a job away from a 'professional mover'. Do we really want to live in a society where guys strong enough to carry sofas, mahogany wardrobes and pianos up and down stairs are out of work and roaming the streets?

➤ Sorry you can't help. You see, as a teen you pulled a practical joke. You emptied out a friend's house while they were away and hid all their stuff in a big barn! But that barn turned out to be the site of an estate auction. Anyway, you can't go near removal lorries for years to come, as a condition of your parole.

➤ The last person you helped move . . . It's a long story and the lawsuit is still pending. There was a lot of breakage and it turned out it wasn't really *their* stuff that you were moving. Anyway, it's best if you don't 'help' with any other 'moving' for now.

UNIVERSAL GET-OUT #2:
THE TEMPORARY PARALYSIS EXCUSE

➤ It sounds extreme, but heavy guilt-tripping requires an equally heavy counterbalance. You need something like Guillain-Barré syndrome, a typically non-fatal disorder causing paralysis that many victims recover from in a few months. If even that's too sick, morbid and not likely to slip by a co-worker or neighbour who sees you every day, there's always Hysterical Paralysis (strictly emotional in onset and duration), which will get you out of not just moving, but giving people rides across town in your new car, too.

Please note: in these situations you do not want to claim strokes, motor neurone disease or serious spine injuries. Not only are these terrible tragedies afflicting millions that you should never mock, but they're too complex to fake.

Getting a Speeding Ticket

You *were* caught driving at 46 in a traffic-calming zone that calls for 25 – but it's midnight on Christmas Eve, there's no one else about and no way you could feasibly do anyone any harm. How do you avoid sharing a cell with scary convicts?

➤ Conjure up every shred of charm you possess, smile sweetly and make a full and heartfelt apology. If they could see it in their heart to let you go with a warning, you'll never do it again.

Request to be sentenced to community service. But you don't have to settle for roadside litter pick-up. Ask for the creative (that is, celebrity) option:

➤ a) Design a video game full of mayhem – but when a player's car enters a traffic-calming zone it slows to a crawl.

➤ b) Produce a suggestive hip-shaking music video about the dangers of speeding.

➤ Your time-release mega-vitamin, time-release antihistamine and time-release antacid all 'went off' at once, causing a surge of energy and making you confuse the accelerator and the brake.

- The Heisenberg Uncertainty Principle states that one cannot simultaneously measure *both* the position and velocity of a sub-atomic particle. Your car, like all physical matter, is comprised of such particles, so clearly the police could not simultaneously determine both its speed and position in a so-called traffic-calming zone. Try not to seem smug about this.

You're about to have a baby! Obviously, this only works if you're a woman; but men, never fear . . .

- Women of any conceivable age should have a pillow or stuffed toy available to shove under their shirt or dress at a moment's notice (see Fig. 1).

Fig. 1

➤ Add a pained expression and a few gasps of agony, and even the most hard-hearted policeman won't be able to resist (see Fig. 2). Lacking a woman faking labour, a man should simply say he's rushing to the nearest hospital where his first-born is due any moment now.

Fig. 2

➤ Offer to start your community service immediately, running a few errands or picking up a take-away for the arresting officer. Warning: some may mistake such thoughtful 'volunteer concierge duty' as a bribe. Imagine!

Stag/Hen Parties and Overseas Weddings

You're generally up for a good night out with your friends but more often than not want to dodge the general debauchery and sobering bar tab that comes with a stag/hen party. You're supposed to be in their wedding party on a distant resort island *and* buy a gift from a wedding list that would've suited Marie Antoinette with a plutonium Amex card. To retain their friendship and your solvency, you need a lacy veil of excuses:

➤ The worst has happened – you've just realized that the stripper at the stag/hen party is your ex. To avoid an awkward scene, you'd better make yourself scarce before that guy/gal with the boom box and Velcro-seamed police/nurse outfit spots you. And to think, they said they were leaving you in order to enter a monastery/convent!

➤ You'd love to invest in a tropical-weight tux/floral backless bridesmaid dress and fly seven hours to tropical Mamagualulu, but every time you even think about getting on a plane you break out in a sweat and have to run off to the nearest bathroom.

Being Reached

Your boss needs you to come in for overtime. Your mum/lawyer/client wants to chat when you've got a romantic evening or sleep-in morning planned. Mobile phones, e-mail, instant messaging and overnight delivery make it ever harder to simply be out of touch. How can you make sure the bell tolls not-right-now for thee?

➥ You got their message a week ago but you were busy and this is the very first chance you've had to get back to them. Remember, the quicker you respond the more people expect it, causing a vicious downward spiral of availability.

➥ You never got their e-mail because of your hyperactive spam filter. You're terribly chagrined and don't know why it would have screened out *their* e-mail in particular. Confide that they wouldn't believe the misspelled come-ons that do get through.

➥ Once you receive an e-mail from someone or about something you're avoiding, create a fake auto-reply: 'I'll be overseas and unreachable until [whatever date sets you free] working with Habitat for Humanity to build thatched dung yurts in Gadzookistan'.

➤ Send a generic reply you'd usually send to your mum – 'Sorry to have been out of touch, just working extra long and hard' – to your boss, and vice versa: 'I'd like to cut back my hours so I can spend more time visiting my parents'. When they catch up with you a day or two later, insist: 'But I got right back to you!'

➤ You had your phone off because you attended the complete *Lord of the Rings* trilogy (10 hours), went straight to an intermission-free *Hamlet* (four hours), then stopped to visit your ailing great-uncle (no phones on the ward!)

UNIVERSAL GET-OUT #3:
BEFRIEND A TECHIE

➤ To avoid being reached, it's crucial to disable features that let message senders detect if you're currently online. This means befriending someone from the IT department at work. They're actually decent folks – except for their *Star Wars* memorabilia fetish. Idly ask your new friend – as you admire their scale-model R2D2 – whether it's possible to forward a specific incoming call to a 'full' mailbox message, or to alter your e-mail's date/time stamp.

➤ Respond to their effort to reach you at a time that you're relatively certain they won't pick up your call or see your e-mail, creating a game of seemingly conscientious tag. To avoid any chance of their picking up and actually talking to you, call from a friend's phone.

➤ It's the old 'I'm too sick to come in to work and if I did I'd give everyone else this awful bug I've got' excuse for the cyber age. You needed to get your PC/mobile phone/Blackberry virus-free before you could respond. It's a viral worm spread through instant messaging, but it can even infect mobile phone calls, sending porn to everyone on the recipient's contacts list.

You didn't get their message because your mobile phone, Blackberry, etc. was utterly ruined after:

➤ a) a taxi drove through a puddle from a broken water main;

➤ b) you dived into a river to save a child and/or

➤ c) you tried that crazy log flume ride!

✗ Expensive Restaurant Meals

They're the youngest person to make partner at Bigg, Staxx, & Kasch. And you? You're in 'the helping professions' or 'an excuse-book writer'. Now they've asked you to dinner at *El Caviarrio*, where picking up the bill could give you a financial hernia. How do you handle it?

▶ Decline their invitation by honestly explaining you're on a tight budget – no need to cite daydreams about selling a kidney to pay off student loans. If they insist on covering your meal, offer to tackle the tip – after all, *you* won't be going back there.

▶ You're *friends*, right? Remind them of life back on Earth. Explain that you may be late because your favourite pawn shop gets busy near mealtimes. Then suggest a nice but more reasonable place around the corner.

▶ Call from your car parked at a cheap take-away two blocks away. Shout over your own honking horn about an impossible traffic jam. You'll make it there in time for dessert – then take them out for a beer at a pub for normal people.

Viewing Holiday Snaps

It may be their encyclopaedic wedding/honeymoon album, a camera-phone full of snapshots from their holiday or a website devoted to their darling new addition. As Bogart meant to say, here's *not* looking at you – or your kids:

→ You're *so* absent-minded! You've left your reading glasses at home and without them everything would just be a blur – and you simply wouldn't be able to do the photos justice. What's that? No, really, no need to describe each photo – you'll do your best to remember your glasses the next time you see them and check out the pics yourself. To make this excuse more believable, try bumping into the odd person as you weave your way off down the street.

→ It has been scientifically proven that for each additional 48 hours you can postpone viewing other people's devastatingly dull photos/videos, you are 10 per cent less likely to ever have to sit through them. So say you don't have the time *right now*. Pick a future date to enjoy them at your leisure, say two weeks from now. And when that date arrives, postpone again. Repeat as necessary until said owner of pics gets the hint.

If they leave their photo album with you and/or e-mail you a link
to an online gallery, you can still skip viewing them if you have
a pleasant comment or two to offer or e-mail back. Here's how
to respond without actually looking:

▶ **Weddings** It looks like it was a beautiful day – I'm sorry
I missed it.

▶ **Birthday** It was great to see you among all your friends.
What a shame I had to work that night.

▶ **Vacation** I feel like I'm seeing that place with a fresh pair
of eyes! The view from where you were staying was
really special.

▶ **Baby** Aw . . . they look just like your merged DNA,
don't they?

▶ **Pet** I've never seen such a lively, yet restful [type of animal].

▶ **New house** That front door looks so *knock*able! And those
windows must let in photons of light! It's like a page from an
estate agent's brochure!

Getting Married

You've been going out for – is it Tuesday? – two years, seven months and three days. Now the 'M' word crops up regularly. Your beloved is gung-ho and you, well . . . you have trouble committing to an extended mobile phone plan. Before being joined in the legal epoxy of holy matrimony, you'd like to mull and procrastinate for another millennium. Here are some rules of disengagement:

➤ You're waiting until the moment is just right: there's currently a seven-month waiting period to have your proposal posted on the stadium scoreboard during your team's next really significant match.

➤ True, your assets amount to a Troll Dolls of the World keychain set, a Complete Women/Men of Tahiti drink coaster set and the dog-stained hand-me-down sofa – but it all needs to be appraised. Then the appraisal has to be notarized, the pre-nuptial agreement drawn up and then . . .

➤ You can't bring yourselves to share your ATM PINs or e-mail account passwords – and that's really bugging you. Sometimes you'll start to say it, but only ******* comes out. How can you be wed while harbouring such secrets?

THE NUCLEAR EXCUSE

Marriage? It's time for The Nuclear Excuse, the painful, only once-spoken truth that must be said really fast and in a single breath.

FOR HIM

→ 'Sorry, but I could never marry a woman who still stacks her bed with fluffy toys, each with its own *special* personality; nor someone who says if I was being burned at the stake during the Dark Ages she wouldn't necessarily speak up and get in trouble herself but she would only pretend to help look for kindling; I realize saying this now instead of a simple "I Do" in front of 150 people who have travelled from three continents is perhaps not the best timing on my part but there you have it.'

FOR HER

→ 'Sorry, but I could never marry a man who refers to his penis as The Little Engine that Could or Thomas the Tank Engine or simply Frodo Baggins; nor someone who when you ask if you look fat in a particular pair of jeans responds, "Compared to what other land and sea mammals?"; I realize saying this now instead of a simple "I Do" in front of 150 people who have travelled from three continents is perhaps not the best timing on my part but there you have it.'

The Art of Extrication or
How to Say 'Gotta Go Now'

The Art of Extrication or How to Say, 'Gotta Go Now'

You didn't act quickly enough or avoidance just didn't work. Now you're trapped in the social equivalent of handcuffs and a straitjacket – plus you're upside-down underwater!

→ You wake up to recall, through a hungover haze, drunkenly sending insulting and/or sloppy sentimental text messages – to your boss.

→ You wake up to the screaming feral children of your unwanted house guests – who've announced they plan to stay on another week.

→ You wake up from a delightful daydream to find yourself still cornered by an endlessly prattling bore at a dismal party – and it seems you're actually that party's host.

The important thing is, you've awakened. Time to swing into action! Sure, the odds seem stacked against you, whether escaping from a romantic relationship without a painfully straightforward conversation or sending an awkward one-night stand packing before breakfast. And it can appear downright impossible to extricate yourself from some angry guy who insists on a fight, from comforting an endlessly teary friend, from the dreary monotony of everyday life or from your own funeral.

This is when you must call upon The Escape Artist Within, that little voice deep down inside, the one that says over and over: 'I'm a devious worm and I can wriggle my way out of anything!' (It's best to keep that little voice to yourself on crowded public transport . . .)

In this section, you'll learn to free yourself from the locked trunk of a romantic relationship with just faux online infidelity and the wrong nicknames. You'll have that one-night stand flying out your door merely by quoting Hitchcock. And you'll liberate yourself from louts, lamenters and last rites with nothing more than nudity, an onion and some chilly liquid nitrogen.

Some escapes require minor preparation – the Santa Switcheroo for bolting from the office holiday parties, or the baby-in-the-bath self-rescue from door-to-door solicitors – but mostly they call for steely determination and relaxed-fit morals, a mindset that insists – *Get Me Out of Here!*

A Blind Date

Mutual friends claimed to know your perfect match. Now you find yourself at the agreed-on café when in walks a sort of Frankenstein (see also: *Bride of*) of social rejects; someone combining bad breath, a Star Trek haircut and orange knitwear in one utterly unappealing package. Fear not, though you walk in the valley of odorous dates, we have your escape routes mapped out:

► The mistaken identity ruse requires quick thinking and an expressionless poker face. Stash any identifying features. (You said you'd be wearing a blue scarf? Reading *The Economist*? Quick, bury them in a bag.) Avoid eye contact and when approached, reply with a regretful, 'No, afraid not . . .' Check your watch and look around before leaving, as though you've been stood up.

► Prearrange for a friend to call you 15 minutes into your date. They say: 'So? What do you think?' You say: 'Oh my God, when?! No, stay where you are, I'll be right there!' Excuse yourself by explaining that you're so sorry, of all times, but there's been a family crisis and/or your best friend is giving birth.

Downside Risk The loser you just met answers their phone first and says, 'Oh my God, when?!'

➤ Plan ahead and take a disguise along with you – a wig, a hat,
a change of clothes, whatever you need to make sure you'll
be unidentifiable. Identify your nearest toilet on arrival
(see Fig. 1).

Fig. 1

◆ Then excuse yourself and
slip into your new
outfit (see Fig. 2).

Fig. 2

◆ Then you should have no problems slipping past your would-be
date and making good your escape (see Fig. 3).

Fig. 3

- Arrive early to scout escape routes. Does the café toilet have a window large enough to climb out? Will you need to fashion an escape ladder from napkins and tablecloths? Can you dart through the kitchen – 'Health inspector!' – and out an alleyway?

  Note: Always have at least two means of evacuation mapped out in case there's a problem with one of them.

- Announce after five minutes of small talk that you're feeling a special bond, a soulmate thing. Do they feel it, too? Ignore their answer. You've only felt this way about one other person, but they cheated on you. Use the toilets. If they're still there when you return, ask who they've chatted up in your absence. Ask if they'd like to keep their options open, blind date other people. If they aren't leaving by then, storm out muttering, 'Et tu, Brute?'

- You've just come from a medical appointment and it turns out you've got a touch – just a touch – of leprosy. The doctor says a two-year course of pills will clear it right up . . . Scratch your wrists violently, then tentatively reach out for his/her hand.

⚊ ESCAPES FOR HIM

THE HYPERSENSITIVE ESCAPE

➤ Confide anecdotes about being 'too soft' in the eyes of your career-military dad. If they raise their hand to signal for the bill, cringe like you're about to be struck.

THE PI-THROWING ESCAPE

➤ Say you really like pi. If she checks the menu, roll your eyes. You mean the *number* 3.14 etc. The ratio of a circle's circumference to its diameter? You can recite it to 500 decimal places!

THE MR SLEAZE ESCAPE

➤ Insist (despite your actual physical appearance) that exes called you 'The Sledgehammer'. Wink. Repeatedly mention your waterbed. Ask if she's ever 'done it' in a dentist's waiting room.

THE VIDEO-GAMING ESCAPE

➤ Which is her favourite? You're into Evil Farmer, where you get to kill off the city slickers building high-rises on your land with a super-laser pitchfork.

ESCAPES FOR HER

THE FAR TOO FRAGILE ESCAPE

➤ Does he like little glass animals? You do so very much! You have a whole menagerie. You realize he hasn't seen them yet, but which one does he expect to like best?

THE TOM-BEAST ESCAPE

➤ You've always wanted a real man, but your last few boyfriends were wet noodles. Ask how long he'd last on a mechanical bull. Suggest arm-wrestling to see who gets the bill. If any of this seems to be appealing to him, segue to talk of glass animals.

THE PRIDE, PREJUDICE AND PETS ESCAPE

➤ Explain within minutes of meeting that you must hurry home to feed your seven cats – Elizabeth, Mr Bingley, Mr Darcy, Mr Wickham, Colonel Fitzwilliam, Lady Catherine de Bourgh and "Kitty" Bennet. If he tries to normalize this – saying you must really love Jane Austen to name all your cats after characters in *Pride and Prejudice* – act taken aback. Insist you don't know any Janes and you can name your own damn cats just fine.

Your Job

When leaving an awful job, giving several weeks' notice only means suffering through a dismal canteen goodbye party and an exit interview where you say it was all great you just need to spend more time with your sofa. Plus, if you quit you won't get the severance and unemployment benefits needed for a nice vacation. Here's how to take extra-early retirement:

➤ Strategically leave a copy of your CV in one or two of the office photocopiers, especially the one that's near the busybody receptionist.

➤ Pretend you've won the mega-jackpot but intend to keep working. During meetings doodle long strings of zeros in your chequebook; hold loud phone conversations in which you discuss Swiss bank accounts and interest accrual. Eventually, for the sake of office morale, you'll be asked to leave.

➤ Prepare a detailed report on how they could send your job overseas for a fraction of what they pay you. Then, ask to combine your performance review where you get a raise for sharp thinking with your exit interview to, again, maximize company savings.

MAKE YOUR JOB DISAPPEAR!
A CHART OF MAGICAL PHRASES

They're not abracadabra but, used routinely, these should convince your employer to set you free:

➤ '. . . whenever I *feel* like it . . .'

➤ '. . . not if I make my presentation first you won't . . .'

➤ '. . . refuse to compromise my commitment to napping . . .'

➤ '. . . We can easily meet that deadline by curving space-time . . .'

➤ '. . . You *said*, "youth in Asia", and I *heard* "euthanasia" so . . .'

➤ '. . . our warranty is meant to set a mood more than anything . . .'

➤ '. . . go ahead and call my supervisor, it's just me using a different voice . . .'

➤ '. . . if our advertised guarantee spoke for itself, it would have a larynx . . .'

➤ '. . . well maybe I find it *inconvenient* . . .'

⚡ The Office Christmas Party

Punch + Co-workers = Danger Zone. Christmas parties bring out a side of your co-workers you'd just rather not know about. So to avoid situations you'll have to pretend didn't happen the next business day, here's how to skip out on the one party you can't skip entirely:

➤ Your boyfriend/girlfriend's company picked the same evening for their party. (A friend can play the role in exchange for all they can eat and drink in 20 minutes.) Complain that you must 'put in an appearance' at that stuffy affair across town.

➤ It's well after normal working hours, perhaps Saturday night, but top management will admire your *business-first!* attitude leading to an early exit with regrets. This works best in fields like computer tech and plumbing. Not so well in, say, pet grooming and dry cleaning. But 'emergency' poodle trims and stain removal requests might still be plausible.

➤ Volunteer to play Father Christmas. You're seen as a team player, putting up with employees' kids tugging your beard and poking your belly. After a photo taken in full regalia with your bosses, switch places with a Rent-a-Santa you've hired and enjoy your evening.

➤ Cover your early exit from a Christmas party at the office by noting that you have one last late shipment for an important client. Stowing yourself away in a large, well-ventilated container, call your pal with that Hallowe'en UPS costume to come and pick you up. (Note: label container with your home address in case, by fluke, a real UPS guy shows up.)

➤ Your deepest apologies for leaving early, but in your religion [name of obscure antibiotic with '-ism' added to end] there is also a winter solstice holiday and there are multiple gods at whose altars you must light candles, leave gift certificates and generally genuflect before. In fact, there's a line-up of twenty-seven of them, so you'd better get a move on.

A Teary Friend

We all have one friend who lives amid perpetual melodrama: lovers always leaving, pets passing weekly and forever getting canned. Sure, they were cheating, their cats are ancient and the jobs are temp gigs, but the forecast is still for streaking mascara and deep drifts of wet tissues. How can you give a nod toward comforting companionship yet get on with your day?

➡ The key to a graceful departure for less gloomy climes is to offer them The Gift of Solitude. After all, they can't properly grieve their lost loser ('. . . *lover,* of course, did I say loser?'), pet or job with you hovering about offering your wan reassurances.

➡ To cut things short, demonstrate an empathy so intense that *they* wind up comforting *you*. Bring an onion and pocketknife, sneak off for some surreptitious slicing, then return teary and red-eyed. Explain that you're just so upset about *their* situation you can't bear it. One last big hug and they'll send you off with solace and tissues.

If your teary friend manages to use up all of their tissues, they'll inadvertently offer you an unmissable escape opportunity.

➤ No bother at all. You'll just dash to the shops and be right back (see Fig. 1).

Fig. 1

Fig. 2

➤ Failing to return (see Fig. 2), you can always explain later that you ran into that lame ex of theirs (and gave them a good talking-to), ran into their ex-boss (ditto) and/or ran over someone else's cat.

➤ You must aid someone else suffering in a similar situation. And this other person is not holding it together anywhere *near* as well. It sounds like a complete gibbering breakdown. This fortifies your teary friend's ego as you head for fun.

UNIVERSAL GET-OUT #4:
THE DRIVING SOMEONE TO A&E ESCAPE

This ace-up-the-sleeve is normally as obvious as a Blind Date Phone Call Escape, but your friend's probably too weepy to notice. Some A&E-worthy ideas:

➤ **Kitchen blender accident** 'I must hurry – at least they've got the fingertips on ice!'

➤ **Medication reaction** 'I must hurry – his erection has lasted more than four hours!'

➤ **Techno-meltdown** 'I must hurry – the DVD player remote "fast-forwarded" their pacemaker!'

Being Dumped

The relationship is winding down, but you're just not ready to be dumped right now, not until you have a Plan B in place and can do the dumping yourself. For such tricky situations we suggest:

➤ Some boyfriends/girlfriends may try leaving their 'it's not you, it's me' speech on your voice mail. Not if you reprogramme it to only accept, say, a 20-second message they won't!

➤ Meet your nearly-ex only in places with electric bands or 110-decibel sound systems. Nothing inhibits a break-up spiel like having to yell it in public. If they try, smile and shrug to indicate you can't hear a word. Afterward? Your ears are still ringing!

Unwanted Advances

The Murphy's Law of being hit on? It's always by the wrong people. At work, a 'stress relief' neck massage comes via the office computer geek. At the gym, the hands-on correction of your form is by a BO-reeking treadmill rat. And the hand on your hip at the bar comes from a staggering mess who spills their fruity drink on you. Here are ways to call off the mangy dogs:

- Delivered with a smile, these lines make it clear that you're not interested. At work: 'Are you trying to type an e-mail? Because that's my neck you've been fingering.' At the gym: 'Thanks for correcting my form, I'll never wash my deltoids again.' At the bar: 'Good thing I'm too drunk to notice you just hit on me and get all freaked out.'

- When it is time to lay down the law . . . At work: 'Maybe in an alternative universe that move's seductive, not just creepy.' The gym: 'Seriously? I'm going to *scrub* my deltoids for hours' The bar: 'There's truly nothing hotter than someone an hour or two from dry retching.'

♦ ESCAPES FOR HIM

THE PERFUME ALLERGY ESCAPE
➤ As she leans in seductively, wrinkle up your face and blink rapidly as if you're tearing up. Explain that you suffer from extreme fragrance sensitivity to perfumes. Clutch your throat and make a wheezing escape.

THE COMMUNICABLE RASH ESCAPE
➤ Grab their wandering hand and ask if they've ever had a rash from eczema. Go off about the terrible itching you're suffering. Invite them to join you in a bath of soothing oatmeal as you scratch at your abdomen with both hands.

THE SHOCKING FAMILY SECRET ESCAPE
➤ If the advancee is someone you've known a while, you can let them down easily by explaining that before your great-aunt Floosianna passed away (they might remember, you had to skip their dinner party to visit her in the hospital) she called you to her bedside and let you in on some family history. She'd had a child by another man, and that child's son/daughter is . . . well, they can work it out. Yes, you explain, we're actually second cousins. So, please, this is just too weird . . .

♦ ESCAPES FOR HER

THE STALKING BRUTAL EX ESCAPE

➤ Tell friends, acquaintances and co-workers about a jealous ex
with an ugly police record and/or an overprotective sibling
whom you rarely see since they joined an élite counter-terrorist
squad. If the guy hitting on you doesn't believe that you have a
pathological ex who wears brass knuckles monogrammed with
your initials or a sister who knows nine ways to kill a man with
his tropical drink umbrella, tell them to ask anyone you know –
or find out for themselves.

THE STATIC ELECTRICITY ESCAPE

➤ Scuff your feet on carpets until you've built up a charge that
stands your hair on end and gives anyone coming too close a
nearly heart-stopping shock. Repeat as necessary.

THE FRAGILITY ESCAPE

➤ 'Thanks for the offer, but my herniated cervical disc means your
clumsy groping neck massage could leave me paralyzed from
the chin down' or 'If you don't mind – I'm *mortally* ticklish –
which tends to set off my asthma!'

This classic escape is a form of misdirection. It's all about making him believe the fiction and then not following through . . .

◆ Pretend you're hot for him (see Fig. 1) and ask him to hook up in the women's washroom (see Fig. 2). Tell him to wait for you in the farthest cubicle.

Fig. 1

◆ Then quickly exit the building, pausing only to inform security there's a creepy guy hiding in the lavatory.

Fig. 2

ESCAPING A DOG'S UNWANTED ADVANCES

When it comes to dogs, 'I think he likes you!' can be five very awkward words. And if he gets any friendlier one of your legs is going to have puppies. This is not the time to roll over.

If its owner won't intervene, here's how to bring that puppy to heel:

➤ **The Squirt in the Snout Escape** Wait until the furry angel's owner turns their back or leaves the room, then a fire off a quick squirt of water at their snout to back them off. Wetting your fingers and flinging the droplets might also work in a pinch. You could also try positive reinforcement by getting him to sit and stay, then feeding him whatever you can get your hands on.

➤ **The Scarecrow Leg Escape** Think of this as putting a chain-smoker on the nicotine patch. If you've faced this hairy humper before, then come prepared with a second pair of trousers or tights. When the dog goes into romantic mode, quickly stuff the spare clothing with throw pillows, blanket, etc. and, like a toreador distracting a charging bull, offer a non-you alternative.

🏃 Public Displays of Affection

Your new squeeze can't keep their hands off you in public. It was sweet at first, but it's beginning to wear on you: the awkward snuggling into the same revolving door compartment, their palm on your buttock while visiting grandpa, the big snogs outside work as your bosses troop by.

Think of lamp-posts and bus shelters not as urban streetscape, but as spatulas for gently prying away your clingy love muffin.

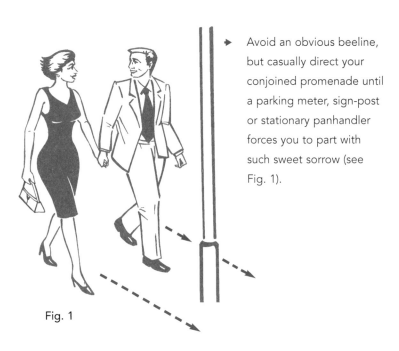

➤ Avoid an obvious beeline, but casually direct your conjoined promenade until a parking meter, sign-post or stationary panhandler forces you to part with such sweet sorrow (see Fig. 1).

Fig. 1

➤ You'll then be free to continue on your way, unhampered by your loved one's affections. Putting your hands in your pockets (see Fig. 2) will help to avoid the situation happening again.

Fig. 2

➤ Insist on aiding the blind, the elderly, children and semi-lame dogs crossing roads and boarding buses. Your flame will understand that you need both hands free, although they may think it odd when you dash back and forth, juggling all four deeds at once.

➤ Sit down (in private), take both their hands in yours and concede that perhaps you're too self-conscious at times. But you're just not sure that your nephew's nursery Nativity play was the right time and place for them to be teething on your earlobe. Prepare to sleep on the sofa for a night or two . . .

➤ Exhaust your beloved in private. Like a boxer who throws all their best punches in the early rounds, they'll stagger outside weak from their exertions, all nuzzled, kissed and groped out. Wear high collars to cover the love-bite that looks like you had heart surgery through your neck.

➤ Consider the mating praying mantis: at first, the male can't get enough of the female. Then she bites his head off – which presumably mellows him out. So, give back double the PDAs you're getting. Are they pinching your bum? Pinch theirs with both hands. Check-out queue kisses? Try face licking.

Work Assignments

Maybe you're a dental hygienist assigned a patient who hasn't flossed in decades. Perhaps you're waiting tables when a notoriously obnoxious-yet-poor-tipping party of seventeen strolls in. Or you work in a shoe shop and a guy with big stinking feet wants help trying on sandals. Don't quit (yet)! Here's how to play hopscotch on the job assignment minefield:

➤ Flatter a more experienced colleague by asking how *they'd* approach the situation. Maintain your befuddlement and ask for a demonstration. As they perform your entire rotten task for you, express deep admiration for their far superior skills.

➤ Mythical hero Hercules had to grab golden apples guarded by a hundred-headed dragon. He convinced Atlas, who had a brutal gig holding up the Earth and the Sky, to go instead as a change of pace. The lesson? Allow the waterlogged dish-washer to wait on that annoying dining party.

➤ To magically elude grim chores, bypass smoke, given most office's restrictions, and go straight to mirrors. One should do the job if it's big enough and aimed at a vacant desk. You can then sit safely out of sight behind it.

Your moral convictions mean you can't take on this task:

➤ It's not that this person hasn't flossed in 20 years. It's that they lie about their dental hygiene régime, which you cannot abide!

➤ You're pretty sure there's something in the Bible about not serving adults who make yackety dolphin-feeding-time-at-the-zoo sounds when you deliver their fish starters.

➤ It just goes completely against your code of fashion ethics to help a big hairy-footed oaf with toenails like sloth claws into a pair of strappy pewter suede designer sandals.

UNIVERSAL GET-OUT #5:
THE GPS YOUR BOSS ESCAPE

➤ Your best bet for escaping heinous gigs is to avoid running into the boss when they've got one to dish out. That means knowing where they are at all times – easy thanks to global positioning devices. Sure, it involves some major risk to routinely plant a high-tech tracking device on your direct supervisor. But next time they have an awful assignment to hand off you'll be nowhere in sight!

A Fight

Maybe you cheered too loudly for the wrong team, booed a punk rocker or spilt your beer on a cranky drunk. Somehow, you've got a maniac suggesting fisticuffs. And he does look like he could bruise a lot more than your ego. Here's how to keep your diet free of knuckle sandwiches:

➤ If you're not fleet of foot, a fast about-face with your tongue is on tap: you were *mocking* the away team, cheering their sad attempts to be competitive! The hulking spiky-haired punk band heard you call them 'talent-free jerks'? You meant their *sound*, it's just like The Talent-Free Jerks, a band from [distant town and/or Iceland] you're crazy about!

➤ If challenged to fight in a pub, try this opening move. Signal to the barman, hand him your credit card and tell him you're buying everyone at the bar a round, maybe more. You now have a horde of people tenderly interested in your well-being.

- The best way to save your skin may be to show it. A quick disrobing should give the most bellicose brawler pause, since he'll figure you're insane. If he still advances, he'll have much less to grab onto. (Hang onto your wallet, as you'll need a cab pronto.)

- Even more effective than stripping – which may not ward off a nasty drunk seeing red – a toss of your cookies should clear a path for your escape. Whether your nemesis warrants the emesis (to use the technical term) is a nauseating judgment call.

- Explain you'd like nothing better than to get physical in a non-Olivia-Newton-John sort of way, but your black belt in Aikijujutsu, a Japanese martial art dating back to the samurai, means that your bare hands are considered deadly weapons and suggest a serious legal liability. So, you'll just be . . . (by now you should be fleeing at full speed . . .)

Turn a potential fracas into a mini-riot by turning your attacker's attention elsewhere:

➤ Act surprised and apologetic when your would-be attacker turns on you, buying time (see Fig. 1).

Fig. 1

As you flee, whack a few other really big guys on their backs as you pass (see Fig. 2).

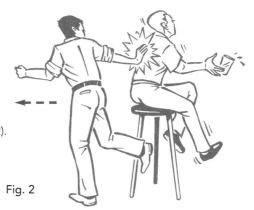

Fig. 2

One or more is bound to mistake your pursuer as the perpetrator and fight your battle for you (see Fig. 3).

Fig. 3

The Aftermath Of
Drunken Behaviour

The word has spread about your dirty dancing with a bar patron twice your age, hitting someone at the pool table with a dizzy dart throw and costly candle globe juggling. Worse? Liberal use of your mobile under the influence. Drink lots of water, take aspirin and apply damage control:

➡ As co-drinkers imitate your table-top dance and howl over the dart toss that gave a pool player rear-end acupuncture, just offer your most bemused Mona Lisa half-smile. Neither admit nor deny anything; let others decide if these are reliable witnesses. If someone has camera-phone proof, you may need to make a 'personal errand-slave' deal.

➡ You sent lots of insulting ('...U R SSINF! U WOMBAT!') or sloppy-romantic ('...QT GmeSumLuvin WAN2:- ?')* text messages? Send out an all-hands e-mail explaining someone stole your phone and apparently sent weird messages via your address book.

First, check for positive responses such as 'I've always had a crush on you, too.'

→ You realize that voice mail *sounds* like you left an obscene
rant, but you were actually backstage rehearsing your big
dramatic monologue in that Mamet play and you must have
bumped your phone in such a way that it speed dialled their
number. Really!

UNIVERSAL GET-OUT #6:
THE WILDER SIBLING

→ All it takes is some PhotoShop work on snapshots, one from
childhood and a more recent picture in business attire: voila!
You and your *identical* twin. Keep the photo framed on your
desk at work and a copy in your wallet for emergency use.
Explain that your bro/sis spends most of his/her time overseas.
They're always off to some exotic locale, then they show up on
your doorstep or at work without warning. And they've always
taken a mischievous delight in pretending to be you! You
almost got into lots of trouble as kids. So, what did they
do *this* time?

Granted, these actions put you over the edge into pathos, but they may be your only out if you've done something truly execrable. Confide that you're taking prescription pills for a minor dyslexia/lactose-intolerance/spleen problem. The label does say never to mix with alcohol because it can, in rare instances, cause psychotic behaviour compounded by short-term amnesia; so, what exactly did you do?

➤ a) Called and woke your ex (or your boss) and rambled on weeping/laughing with sentiment/obscenity.

➤ b) Passed out back at your desk in the foetal position without your trousers on.

➤ c) Woke up with your direct supervisor/that person more than twice your age you danced with/the pool-table man-beast you hit with a dart.

An Orgy

A friend of a friend invites you to 'an intimate gathering' but it turns out that wearing trousers makes you overdressed for the occasion. You consider yourself sexually liberated, but this is *not* your thing. Besides, the assembled group looks like an X-rated version of the bar scene in *Star Wars*. How do you suavely skip out on a *ménage à douzaine*?

- Insist that everyone there has to play Six Degrees of My Sleazy Ex-Brother-In-Law Ray. (This should buy you time to escape through a bathroom window.)

- You're allergic to latex!

- You have this major hang-up – you can only have group sex with a *prime* number of people.

- You've always considered a hot tub packed with naked people to be 'human soup' – and you're vegetarian.

- You kind of like to be wined and dined first – which means, 7, 8, 9 . . . *twelve* dinners!

- You just wouldn't feel right cheating on your Tuesday night sex group.

The Scene of a One-Night Stand

It was major beer goggles or lust at first sight that's left you queasy with second thoughts. The point is: you've got to leave fast (or get this ludicrous lover out of *your* house) with assurances that it was really great and/or nothing to be ashamed of. You'll call them – and this time by their correct name! – really soon. Here's how to get out of there quick-smart:

▶ Sorry to skip breakfast, but your Sex Addicts Anonymous meeting starts in ten minutes. As for lunch, your Genital Warts and Herpes Support Group is having a picnic to celebrate 30 days without a major visible outbreak. But you'll definitely stay in touch!

▶ Discreetly set your watch forward eight hours, then bolt from bed, hastily grabbing your clothes and pointing out the time in Beijing/Dubai/The Hague. It's dawn here but late afternoon over there and you've got a major currency deal to close!

➤ Sneak around picking up your clothes while humming the Pink Panther theme. Cartoonishly exaggerate the stealth: move on tip-toe, knees raised high, hands held aloft with wrists stiffly bent. If they wake and catch you preparing to leave before dawn, you can pretend you were just goofing around and hurry back to bed. Once they nod off – repeat.

➡ Oops! Your still-infatuated ex is returning on the early flight this morning from their Ninja Death Match Tournament abroad. You're picking them up at the airport to check out their first-place medal – supposedly a gold-plated human ear! Sorry to miss breakfast!

➡ You've got a full-grown Great Dane at home. If you don't hurry back to take him out for his morning ritual, your place won't be habitable for months.

➡ You've already lied about your job's glamour to get them in the sack – meat-slicing at a deli counter became 'veterinary surgeon' – so now that there's an emergency they'll understand that you must run to the aid of an injured thoroughbred. Next time, however, a VIP breakfast is definitely on you!

➡ Wake them at daybreak and ask if they've ever heard of the Code Delta Force. Your real name isn't Michael/Kate, but that's not important now. You must leave right away. No time for breakfast, and they certainly can't tag along where you're going.

IF THEY'RE AT *YOUR* PLACE

THE CLERICAL/RABBINICAL ESCAPE
- Don a collar or habit left over from Hallowe'en, say you'll treasure the memory but your vows rule out repeats. If it's Saturday, pin a fabric coaster in your hair and explain you've got to run – you're presiding over the Greenblatt bar mitzvah in an hour.

THE PSYCHO ESCAPE
- Slip into another room – a closet will do – and fake an early morning argument with someone unseen. Return to bed and explain that your mum lives with you and 'She just goes a little mad sometimes'. If they aren't a) sufficiently creeped out or b) recognizing that you're quoting Hitchcock, lay it on thicker: 'Oh, but she's as harmless as one of those stuffed birds, etc.' Continue until they turn down your shower offer and hurry away.

THE SURPRISE ENDING ESCAPE
- That was terrific, but another 'client' is arriving at 9 AM so you've got to get cleaned up. Wink and add: 'Last night was so good, let's say it's on the house.'

Unwanted House Guests

You've had weekend visitors – friends with out-of-control kids, old pals who were too loud too late and/or pernickety relatives who disparaged your housekeeping. You thought the worst was over, but now they're talking about staying a few more days. How do you get them out of here?

➡ Rise early to prepare a hearty 'final morning' breakfast. Point out that it's a lovely day to travel. Set the table with lovingly stitched needlework place mats quoting Benjamin Franklin to the effect that fish and visitors both stink after three days.

➡ Appear at breakfast with a packed suitcase. You didn't think they'd still be around, so exterminators are coming today to absolutely *bomb* the place. You're so glad that the bedbugs, roaches and black widows didn't bother them during their stay.

➡ The police think some awful business may have occurred here before you moved in. They're coming today to dust for prints, spray something that reveals blood residue and rip up floorboards to see if anything – or anyone – is secreted in the crawl spaces.

➤ You hope they've enjoyed their stay, but you've rented out their room to tourists who arrive today. Of course, your plausibility may vary: Victorian cottage in historic district, easy; shabby apartment next to motorway slip road, hard.

➤ While it requires the sort of poker face usually available to normal people only via extensive Botox injections, this may be the most satisfying of house guest ejections. While they're out, you hurl their belongings around the spare bedroom and/or toss them out of the window. You could also routinely awaken them in the wee small hours by randomly pounding on the floorboards with a broom handle and/or playing *The Dark Side of the Moon* with speakers pressed against their wall and the bass pushed up to '10'. Explain that your home's haunted by an obnoxious spirit who seems to have little patience with longer-term guests.

You have other guests arriving:

➤ a) Friends coming into town for an annual snake and spider swop meet.

➤ b) Your ex with their new lover. As you know better than anyone, they can get bit 'noisy' at night.

A Dismal Party

The drinks are watery, the dip runny and the music too loud yet impossible to dance to. Among the few people who showed up there's not a soul you'd consider flirting with. Sure, your escape may be harder if you're the host, but do yourself a party favour anyway:

➤ You're just going to the corner shop and will be right back. Of course, you won't return. If you're ever asked, have a surreal excuse-story ready: you ran into Jane Goodall! Not the world-famous chimpanzee expert, your childhood sweetheart, *that* Jane Goodall. (Women may opt for Tim Berners-Lee, 'not the guy who invented World Wide Web . . .')

➤ If you're a woman, approach any single guy by himself and run your finger along his neck while whispering 'Let's get out of here'. (See Fig. 1)

Fig. 1

◆ A long shot? Scientific research shows it works 97.4 per cent of the time (see Fig. 2).

Fig. 2

◆ Dangerous? Quite possibly. Once the guy has escorted you to your car, it is time to make your excuses (see Fig. 3). See: Escaping from a Blind Date, p. 60 for your next step.

Fig. 3

IF IT'S YOUR OWN PARTY . . .

THE RELOCATION TO A BAR ESCAPE

➤ Sadly announce that neighbours have complained about the noise. Suggest that the whole group adjourn to a nearby pub. And the first round's on you! Once at the bar, pay the tab and find a better party.

THE CAMERA-PHONE SCAVENGER HUNT ESCAPE

➤ Provide a list of stuff they'll need to snap and e-mail you. The first four things are in your home. The next three just outside. The next two inside a cab or bus. The last one is way across town. When they've submitted all ten you'll text them where to find their prize. Having sent your guests away, be decent and hide some champagne at the hunt's end.

THE FAUX SURPRISE ESCAPE

➤ For when you just don't care. Buzzing someone in from downstairs, announce that it's actually their birthday. After everyone hides, douse the lights and crack the door. Once the big 'Surprise!' is launched upon the confused latecomer, all will look for you to explain, but under cover of darkness and commotion you've sneaked out the back.

Plant and Pet Care,
House-sitting and Babysitting

You owe someone a favour because they helped you fix a flat tyre in the rain, gave you a late-night lift home or pretended to be your possessive date (so you *couldn't* dance with Dave/Tina at the office party). But now they're asking you to take care of their botanical garden, care for five cats, keep an eye on their place or baby-sit. Here's how to take a stand against sitting:

➤ You know you owe them, but a temporary conflict gives you another turn at the Wheel of Favours. You'll pay off your moral debt at a cheaper rate if you can delay until: a) you've both forgotten their original favour or b) they ask you to pick up a take-away.

➤ 'Involuntarily' shudder, then confide that you suffer from botanophobia (fear of plants), felinophobia (fear of cats), copro-felinophobia (fear of cat poo) and paedophobia (fear of children). For good measure you can throw in felino-paedo-pediophobia (fear of kids' cat dolls). Reel this off while wringing your hands and taking nervous shallow breaths.

UNIVERSAL GET-OUT #7:
THE DEMONSTRATED IRRESPONSIBILITY ESCAPE

➤ It may not always seem 'cool', 'classy' or 'sane' to have a
window box or flowerpot brimming with beyond-dead greenery.
Indeed, it will take extra work and money to buy plastic shrubs
and silk flowers, then carefully stain and tear them to achieve a
permanent post-locust look. But think of the time you'll save,
not caring for someone else's plants and garden.

Likewise, framed pictures of short-lived pets (Rex 'November
1996–March 1997' 'He's the Lord's Problem Now') should ward
off sitting requests. If someone still asks you for childcare, they
should be reported to the proper authorities.

➤ Unfortunately, your biological responses won't allow you to
help. Ask what kind of dog/cat/bird/plants they need cared for.
Then explain with a sad shake of the head that you are violently
allergic to [specific type of dog/cat/bird/plants they just named,
slip in 'non-related children' if necessary]. Learn to say the
phrase 'terrible rash and potentially life-threatening anaphylactic
shock' so that it rolls off your tongue as easily as 'I almost had
to sit Ed/Edwina's dog, let's grab a pint.'

THE NUCLEAR EXCUSE

The spoken-on-one-breath truth, conveyed with one foot already
out the door.

➤ 'Sorry, I've done some maths and you can count me out. I don't
think that fixing a flat tyre (really you just held the wheel nuts
and umbrella) is anywhere near the equivalent of sifting reeking
cat poo then opening cans of gag-inducing liver-in-sauce while I
kick away your yowling pests rubbing up against me like
perverts on a rush-hour bus. A few more taps on the moral
calculator reveals that a lift home (you were going my direction
anyway and hoping to get asked in for tea) does not equal
three or four visits to your musty flat in support of your Little
Shop of Horrors rainforest plant fetish or checking to see that
some diabolical burglar isn't on eBay giddily auctioning off your
collection of airport gift-shop world capitals snow globes or
margin-scribbled Harry Potter hardbacks. As for pretending to
be my jealous lover at the office party, not even *that* plus the
promise of a future kidney donation is worth an evening stuck in
the broken-toy-strewn eighth circle with your sticky-fingered
snot-nosed impulse-disordered hyperactive demon child.'

🏃 Losing the Party Bore

Like a barnacle on a yacht hull, the dullest person at the party has latched onto you. They're talking non-stop about computer upgrades, their mum's hip surgery or their new hobby, building miniature replicas of nuclear power plants. You finally understand the phrase 'bored to tears'. Time to act!

➤ Snag a passerby and say, 'Hi Chris! [insert dullard's name] here is telling me all about post-surgical sponge baths, didn't you have to do that?' 'Valerie! Didn't you just upgrade your PC? How *crazy* was that?' Eventually, someone will mistakenly venture an opinion – now *they* are trapped in the bore's web of tedium and you can use the brief distraction to dart away.

➤ Same as above, but to end the cycle of victimization gather as many innocent bystanders into the orbit of you and this lightless sun as you can. Eventually, the volume and variety of chatter will, by natural evolution, steer the group's conversation away from computer code customization and back to who's sleeping with whom, bizarre celebrity news and the last party where you all got really drunk together. The Bore will eventually drift off, in search of new victims.

◆ Say, 'Sounds like building scale-model nuke plants is downright addictive! But listen to me! I could talk about this all night but I've got to make sure the rest of these potted plants are properly watered.' This may seem odd if the party isn't yours, but hurry off before that issue gets raised.

If you happen to bump into the Party Bore at some point in the evening, use this tried and tested technique to get rid of them again:

◆ Look pleased to see them, clap them on the shoulder and ask them immediately if they know where the toilet is (see Fig. 1).

Fig. 1

Fig. 2

If they do know, tell them they're a godsend and elegantly turn your clap on the shoulder into a lever as you sweep past them and head for the door (see Fig. 2).

If the party is at your house, this excuse may look a little thin. In this case, ask them where so-and-so (such as your wife) is. Rush off swiftly on a task of great importance, leaving them confused and bewildered (see Fig. 3).

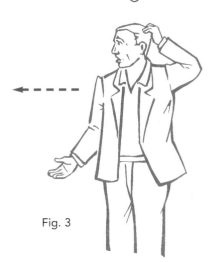

Fig. 3

- Point out someone across the room – anyone they don't know – and suggest they'd be the perfect person with whom to discuss scale-model power plants. Apparently, they built a natural gas refinery out of pipe cleaners and ice-lolly sticks and it won some sort of prize for its detail. Say that you'll rejoin their conversation in just a moment, then make your heart-pounding dash back to freedom.

  If you run into the tiresome talker later, admit you stand corrected: 'You're right, they didn't build that model, but I think I know who did. Let me just go look for them.'

- Apologetically interrupt and ask if they believe in love at first sight. Point at someone across the room and whisper, 'Wish me luck!' Hurry over to the stranger and/or old friend you'd never date and ask, 'Do you think it's possible to be bored to death?'

⚐ A Romantic Relationship

You've decided your relationship needs to end. Everything you used to find delightful now makes you feel homicidal. When you need to generate major loopholes in your implied romantic contract, here are your best moves:

➤ Sit down face-to-face someplace where you won't get interrupted but can quickly exit. (For example, International Space Station, bad. Park bench, good.) Explain in a clear, firm voice that you've had a change of heart, it's not them it's you and that you wish them the best . . . (adding in muttering aside) with the next poor soul they afflict.

➤ Insist on answering mobile calls whenever. No matter how intense the conversation, in the middle of sex, etc. Choose the humpback whale flatulence ring-tone. Programme the phone to ring frequently or hire a professional service to call constantly.

➤ Cultivate a strong sense of mistrust. Example: at restaurants, take big bites of their food while they're using the toilets, then insist – with their meal's residue prominently wedged in your gums – that you have no idea what they're talking about.

➤ You're planning on a tattoo. A whole-body circus freak number: 'It'll take all my savings and hurt like hell, but I'll carry an accurate, complete, topographical map of Middle Earth with me to my grave.' A temporary henna sample, dabbed with fresh ketchup, should send them packing.

A roving eye is nothing to apologise about. Cultivate one and then turn it up a few notches . . .

➤ Give a long sideways glance and emit a low whistle every time an attractive person of their gender goes by. Insist you're *just looking* (see Fig. 1).

Fig. 1

→ Gradually reduce your discrimination threshold until you're ogling statues, garden gnomes and saucily crawling bugs (see Fig. 2).

Fig. 2

Now that you're so comfortable together in bed you'd like to:

→ a) Pretend you're both kangaroos – wearing front-facing bumbags stuffed with fluffy toys and hopping around the bedroom.

→ b) Pretend you're both praying mantises. Insist on being the one who suddenly bites the other's head off.

→ c) Pretend they're applying for a mortgage. Keep asking them about credit rating and income documentation as things progress.

THE CHART OF RAPID ROMANTIC RUINATIONS

FOR HIM	FOR HER
Never shave or remove any hair. From any body part. Ever.	Never shave or remove any hair. From any body part. Ever.
Assure her that you think her breast size/symmetry is just fine – constantly.	Assure him that you really don't mind that he's losing his hair – constantly.
Fill your medicine cabinet with half-empty herpes creams/pills and insist, 'They're leftovers from ex-girlfriends, never used 'em myself'.	Fill your medicine cabinet with half-empty containers of yeast infection creams or pills and insist that he shouldn't worry his 'cute little rapidly-balding head' about it.
Nicknames for her: 'My latest', 'Ball & Chainiac', 'Queen of the Damned', 'The Hague', 'Attila My Honey'.	Repeatedly refer to him by the nickname that you told him you'd given to your vibrator.
When you're sent out to buy tampons come back with beer instead.	When you're sent out to buy beer, just never come back.

Unwanted House-Callers

You bound to the front door expecting a vital delivery. Instead, it's a politely insistent coterie of Jehovah's Witnesses spreading the good word. (This week's topic: 'Disappointments on Our Doorstep: Where Do We Seek Comfort?') Or perhaps it's someone painfully earnest, selling kitchenware, cosmetics or encyclopaedias. Maybe you grab your ringing phone expecting a friend's callback, but no, it's a charity or political fund-raiser. (You agree on the urgent need, it's just, well, *money*, right?) You don't want to seem disrespectful, unkind or ungenerous, you just want to become instantly invisible and unavailable. In the absence of a Harry Potter cloak, we've got your means of egress right here:

- If you're a guy, quickly squeeze into a wife or girlfriend's cocktail dress (the bad fit is a plus) before answering the door. If you're a woman, apply raccoon mascara and lipstick that surrounds your mouth like the rings of Saturn and extends to one ear. Slap at imaginary bugs on the door frame, stare fearfully at their feet or squint as though you haven't seen the sun in days while asking 'Who *really* sent you?!' This should quickly send even the most fervent solicitors back-pedalling, explaining that they have 'the wrong address'.

A surreptitious and spy-like escape out the back door coupled with a re-entry sequence will have callers confused for weeks:

◆ On hearing a knock at the door (see Fig. 1), glance out the window or peephole and assess the threat (see Fig. 2).

Fig. 1

→ Then quickly exit out your back way. Besides not answering your door, this escape lets you pre-empt return visits.

Fig. 2

→ Walk round the front and address the people on your doorstep as if you're just Mr/Ms Neighbour Passing By (see Fig. 3). Try 'They work the night shift at that big gun factory, so they are probably sleeping', or 'You'll be waiting a while. The person who lives there just got sent to prison'.

Fig. 3

THE TELE-EJECTION PHRASE LIST

If you had Caller ID or glanced at it you'd never have picked up the phone. But it's not too late to make this call a quick one. Just cut out the following, have it laminated and keep it right next the phone along with emergency and take-away pizza phone numbers. Be sure to alternate your lines so their delivery stays fresh:

- '. . . you've reached my mobile. I can't talk while driving because I get dis–' (scream, abruptly hang up)

- '. . . you've caught me with the runs, let me just switch to the phone over by the toilet . . .'

- '. . . what a coincidence, you've reached another call centre, I'm recording this to ensure quality service . . .'

- '. . . [smash a magazine down next to mouthpiece] Sorry about that, bit of a cockroach problem. So, you were saying? . . .'

- '. . . I'd know that voice anywhere, did you go to [your school]? . . . I *know* it's you, how'd you wind up doing *this*? . . .'

- '. . . this isn't one of those scary bits where it winds up you're calling me from inside my own flat is it?'

Doing Housework

You agreed with your spouse, roommate or live-in to take turns doing the dishes, dusting, mopping, hoovering and bathroom scrubbing – but after a full day of work you feel a state of Zen detachment from such mundane worldly squalor. You can't skip your share entirely, but here's how to sweep a bunch under the carpet:

- Negotiate a peace treaty dividing your home into public zones for visitors that require serious cleaning and private areas, where chaos may reign. If you're not the cleaning type, the goal is to limit guests to the living room, dining area, and one bathroom.

You were not 'napping instead of cleaning', you:

- a) slipped on a banana peel that fell out of the kitchen rubbish, bruised your coccyx and passed out from the pain.

- b) unclogged the sink with a plunger, which suddenly popped loose hurling you backward onto the armchair.

- c) were trying to finally toss out that old souvenir boomerang, but it circled back and whacked you on the back of the head.

- It's true that the living room still has teetering stacks of old pizza boxes, CDs, DVDs and magazines, but you removed all the unused icons on your shared 'desktop' and then emptied the 'recycling bin', so you're making progress.

- It may not *look* like you cleaned up very much, but you've cleared a precise path among the Lego, dirty socks and old magazines, generating a contemplative clockwise maze that aligns your home's flow of chi life-force with both the fire sign (spicy snacks) and the water sign (the hot tub).

- Dust, mould and cleaning-fluid fumes can give some people fits. If you failed to make this excuse initially you'll need to get busy with fake wheezing.

- After paying a professional cleaner to come and do your share, confide that you have an old friend that your partner's never met who suffers from an overpowering need to clean. It's one of those conditions that usually responds well to medication, but there's an occasional setback – it's a chemical imbalance. He/she is coming for a visit tomorrow and if they should happen to show up in some sort of 'maid' outfit and start wiping the place down, just act like it's the most normal thing in the world.

Volunteer Work

In a moment of weakness you agreed to do volunteer work for an undeniably worthy cause: picking up litter at a local park, sorting used clothing at a homeless shelter or answering a crisis hotline. But the day has arrived and your latest squeeze has tickets to a concert, there's a marathon showing of your favorite sitcom on TV and/or you've got a hangover that even the strongest coffee won't dent. Here's how to get out of doing good:

➤ Just as you might be able to leave your regular job early if you get everything done ahead of schedule, so you should aim to get your volunteer work done in half the time. Don't think of it as giving short shrift, think of it as being more voluntarily productive. For example, if you're picking up litter in a park, concentrate only on those items that will never biodegrade.

➤ It has struck you that perhaps your volunteer work could undermine the self-motivation and dignity of those you're trying to help: don't certain birds use cigarette ends, sweet wrappers and other park litter to build better nests that attract mates, so aren't you dooming a bunch of decent single-but-looking birds by picking it up? Certainly, you'll need some time to think this over before you can whole-heartedly participate.

Unless you're working for Habitat for Humanity using big hammers and saws, there's not usually that much you can do to hurt yourself while volunteering – unless you really try:

- Stuffing envelopes to solicit donations: third-degree paper cuts.

- Visiting the homebound elderly: allergic reaction to stuffy rooms.

- Sorting used clothing at a shelter: lung obstruction from inhaled pocket lint.

While it's definitely harder to get fired from volunteer work than from your regular job, you can still bring your experience from the for-profit sector into play:

- Incompetence: when ladling out sustenance in a soup kitchen, routinely miss the bowls.

- Poor customer service: when manning a crisis hotline, ask if they can call back later as you're in a bit of funk yourself having to volunteer on such a nice day.

- Too slow: when picking up park litter, use tongs to place each cigarette end into its own little bag.

The Dreary Monotony of Everyday Life

So your day goes something like this: morning bathroom routine. Eat mega-fibre cereal. Wait in traffic, wait for download, replace printer toner, ride lift with someone humming off-key. Sit in meetings. Grab lunch at coffee-chain with a million identical set-ups. Call 'busy' friend; avoid a bore by saying you're busy. Read 'crazy' e-mail sent to you at work. Pick up dry cleaning. Jog on treadmill. Eat cereal for dinner. Web surf. Channel hop. Stop! Here are exit options from zombiehood:

→ Shake up everything. Commute by skateboard. Wear your watch on the 'wrong' wrist. Go to zoos on lunch hour and get licked by exotic species. Make meeting comments in iambic pentameter. Volunteer at an ante-natal class – and a hospice. Study ancient martial arts – and harmonica. Grow some of your own food. Or just triple your coffee intake.

→ Have dinner for breakfast. If possible, work different hours or days. Work until 1 AM Saturday, spend Tuesday afternoon in a dodgy bar. Go bat-watching and do solar astronomy. Eat different colour foods based on the day of the week. Use a traditional Bangladesh calendar: celebrate New Year on the first of Boishakh, Pôhela Boishakh (14 April).

➤ Hire a stylist. And a web designer. Create the ultimate MySpace profile. Add a self-promoting blog. Make 'appearances'. Hire a publicist. Set up a red carpet to the front door of your studio apartment. Hire a paparazzo or two to follow you – to get the ball rolling. Develop press leaks. Deny romantic links with other celebrities. Randomly lunge at a paparazzo. Use your web page to 'set the record straight' about your wee-hours hot-tubbing with theoretical physicist Stephen Hawking and daily snorting of crushed Ritalin pills followed by marathon pool-side spelling bees with your thesaurus-toting entourage. And so on.

- Start a weird benign rumour and do everything you legally can to spread it. Examples: Swiss cheese holes spell stencilled messages in Braille. Dalmatians have been cross-bred with zebras to create huge dogs bearing hairy exclamation marks. You can set off airport metal-detectors by thinking about pots and pans. Mention it to gossips. Post it on bulletin boards. Start a blog about it. Chart the Google citations and the major media echoes.

- Why not 'You: The Movie'? With iPods holding 15,000 songs, you've got an instant soundtrack. Add narrow glasses to put everyday life in DVD widescreen 'letterbox' format. Mull camera angles. Finish meetings and meals by shouting, 'That's a wrap!'

- With permission, borrow your own or someone else's verbal six-year-old every few days and ask them to lead you around, blindfolded, while they describe what you're missing. Then walk the same route yourself after they've gone off for their nap.

Your Own Funeral

An open casket could add insult to your biggest injury ever: 'Whoa, is he wearing rouge and lipstick?' 'Actually, she looks good, considering . . .' And if you're into reincarnation, there's a certain been-there-done-that aspect. Here's how to go from 'dearly departed' to 'later, dude'.

➤ Insist on cryopreserving your body at temperatures as low as minus 196°C. The thinking is that centuries from now science will advance enough to revive you. The sheer indignity of your survivors gathering around a steel tank of liquid nitrogen holding your remains like a frozen fish finger should can any memorial service. When they find out you've put all of their inheritance towards paying for the chilling bill, your ceremony will be put on hold until you revive and croak again.

➤ Outlive everybody – granted, a bit tricky given the role of genes and the environment. However, you can do your bit. Don't smoke. Pursue weight-bearing and cardiovascular workouts, eat low-fat, high-fibre, omega-3-laden meals, practice stress reduction and safe regular sex in a mutually supportive emotionally committed relationship. Sure, some rotten thing will get you anyway, but by then, everyone you knew will be long gone, so you can skip having a funeral.

➤ Hold your funeral while you're still alive. Eulogize the 'old you' – that smoking overweight disorganized procrastinator. Cremate your last smokes. Bury your 'relaxed fit' shower curtain and never-opened 'Habits of Organized Persons' calendar. Also declare dead your dreams of movie stardom, sports fame and/or becoming a celebrity chef. Then hold a great big party. By the time your real funeral rolls around, it'll be too redundant to bother.

➤ Fake your own death. Overlook the creepiness, blatant illegality and the conspiracy theories that may eventually follow. Think of it as giving friends and family – informed beforehand, so they're not upset – a golden escape option. Yes, everyone you know can get out of bad blind dates, pathetic parties, boring business meetings, hellish housework, lame dancing, horrid house guests and one-night stands gone awry. Officially speaking, they've got a funeral to go to!

Index